How to Analyze People

Reading People, Body Language,

Recognizing Emotions & Facial Expressions

Bradley Fairbanks

Table of Contents

Introduction

I want to thank you and congratulate you for downloading the book, "How to Analyze People: Body Language and Facial Expressions".

Have you ever wished you could read minds, or at least that you could understand what people were truly feeling and thinking? This information doesn't always come easily, so it's useful to get better at analyzing people, reading them, and deciphering body language. When you hone this skill, you can tell when someone is annoyed, happy, lying, or thinks favorably of you. Why are these skills helpful?

Benefits to Reading People

- ***Professional Benefits:*** *Reading people is very useful in the realm of jobs and careers. In order to know how to pick the best employees, this is necessary. Whether you are a manager who needs to direct employees, a customer service representative, or simply interviewing for a job position you hope to get, this will help you.*

- **Social Advantages:** *We all know that one person who seems to be the center of attention everywhere they go and lights up the room with their charisma. These types of personalities are typically great at reading social cues and body language and using this information to their advantage. Someone who is charismatic and well-liked knows how to analyze people, read them, and respond in favorable and appropriate ways. In other words, learning this skill will help you immensely in your social life.*

- **Closer Relationships:** *When you can read what someone truly feels and thinks, you can improve at giving them what they want. When it comes to relationships (especially romantic ones), this is a must for deepening a bond that will last a long time. Some people get into fights with their spouse or significant other and can't fix it because they don't know what to do. When you know how to effectively analyze and read people, problems like this become a thing of the past.*

As you can see, you'll be missing out on a lot of great benefits by not learning this skill. In this book, you will learn more about why it's so important to read people, which cues and physical gestures mean, and how to tell if someone likes you or is lying to you. As soon as you're done reading this material, you'll be able to recognize signals and communicate much more effectively. Congratulations on taking the time to learn such a valuable skill.

Why Body Language Matters

If your hope is to learn how to read people, you need to learn about body language and nonverbal communication. What these concepts mean is basically communicating without using words, or rather, the communication that exists in addition to simply the words being used. This can mean anything that a person does that another person interprets in a certain way. Not every sign that a person is sending is on purpose, so oftentimes, they are misinterpreted or simply missed altogether and not recognized. Nonverbal communication is subtle, complicated, and multifaceted. It can be structured when you follow specific rules, but most of the time it isn't very structured.

Why is this Topic so Fascinating to us?

It's no mystery why people are so interested in the subject of nonverbal communication and body language.

- ***An Everyday Need:*** *Everyone is a natural people watcher who seeks to understand the psychology of those around them. This is because it's a necessity to be this way. In all aspects of work, including meetings or interactions with the boss or co-workers, observing people is important. We evolved to have this skill, but some of us in this distracting modern age have* *lost it. In this book, you will learn how to get back in touch with your innate instincts, intuitive body reading abilities, as well as learn some brand new skills you never would have thought of before.*

- **Functioning in the World:** *Due to being adults, everyone is skilled at deceit. This isn't always a negative thing. Presenting ourselves in ways that are socially acceptable is necessary to protect people's feelings and to get ahead in this world. CEOs and politicians are even trained by professional actors to learn how to be presentable. This is because they are aware that although they have talented speech writers, the way they deliver what they say is just as important as the words they use.*

Experts are known to analyze and record speeches to decipher movements in the face or body to find evidence that the person speaking is lying or being deceptive in some way. Every actor is aware that nonverbal cues are important to master in order to play a character believably. Even the simplest of gestures, when magnified and exaggerated, can make clear who the actor is supposed to represent. This is because body language is a strong signal, whether we are consciously aware of it or not.

Being Unaware of Body Language

Some people think the messages sent by another person's physical stances or gestures are more reliable than what they say. After all, we are always sending these cues and signals whether we know we are or not. These signals are then either noticed by others or not. At times, we may subconsciously feel something, while we consciously have a very different opinion. For these reasons, it's important to notice speech in conjunction with nonverbal cues, in order to get a fuller picture of the truth.

What do Nonverbal Cues do?

There are a lot of reasons why we use nonverbal behavior, including important social functions. Here are some of the key ways that nonverbal cues are used in everyday social interactions:

- **To Emphasize:** The body language gestures a person makes as they speak or listen can indicate that they are interested, enthusiastic, angry, or some other strong emotion. For instance, if someone is telling an exciting story and pacing around gesturing wildly, they seem much more enthralled and believable than someone who simply sits and quietly speaks without much emotion.

- **To Intentionally Confuse:** Some people use conflicting body language in order to intentionally deceive others. For instance, they might tell you that something is okay while clearly displaying body language that shows that they are *unhappy with it (a clear sign of passive aggression and manipulation.)*

- **To Insinuate:** *Some messages are better left unsaid and only insinuated with nonverbal cues. For instance, if someone is trying to convey a hidden message while tell a story, it's better to simply make a facial expression that gets this message across. When someone is telling a funny story but doesn't want to directly give away what they are saying, we use body language reading to understand them, and to show them how we feel about what they are saying. As you can see, we use this skill intuitively and often without even thinking twice about it.*

Nonverbal cues can be either very obvious, or so subtle that they are easily missed. They can also be consciously given or unconsciously read. At times, it can be an enemy, if it reveals something about yourself that you were trying to keep private, but it can also help you send messages intentionally. Movements of the head, face, tone of voice, and other body gestures all send signals all the time. As you can see, it's all in the way you use this information. One only has to think about the concept of silent movies in order to understand how strong this is in humans. They use punctuation marks, numbers, and gestures in order to indicate meaning.

Where does Body Language Come from?

Most human traits come from either natural instincts or learned responses; in other words, nature or nurture. It's very hard to figure out which is which when it comes to nonverbal behaviors. We learn from our parents and at school what is okay and what isn't as far as eye contact, gestures, and physical touch socially. But is this something we are born with, or something we are taught?

Evidence that Body Language is Instinctual

Here are some reasons that body language could be naturally ingrained in us rather than something we are taught by our families and society.

- *Deaf and blind children still show behaviors such as frowning, nodding, and smiling, even if they haven't been explicitly taught them. These are natural skills that we are born with no matter who we are and what our life circumstances are like.*

- *Brand new babies show familiar emotions such as interest, surprise, pain, or joy. They begin to mimic the expressions of their mothers shortly after being born, as well. They seem to sense this and go along with it right away, without the need to be taught or trained in it.*

- *Twins who grew up not knowing each other have shown very similar tendencies like movements of the head and general posture. This suggests that these inclinations we have to act certain ways have a lot to do with natural instincts that* developed throughout evolution and human advancement and development.

- Studies across different cultures have proven that humans express feelings in very similar ways, such as sadness, happiness, anger, surprise, and more) in addition to easily recognizing them in each other. Simply being human is enough to have these tendencies. In addition, our primate relatives show similar ones.

Body language communication has to do with all of the signals and signs involved with sensory, vocal, and visual input systems we are born with. Nonverbal cues are there to reinforce, replace, and at times (as mentioned earlier) to intentionally confuse or contradict spoken words. These cues could simply and easily stand in the place of verbal cues for answers like "yes", "no", or "maybe." Sometimes, body language signals can exaggerate, underline, or stress verbal messages. But body language signals can also cancel out verbal signals, as mentioned before.

The Evolutionary Development of Body Language

Nonverbal communication has an obvious biological foundation and is the result of our species evolving and developing. It has developed along with us as a way to accurately read each other and cooperate.

- **Comparing it to Animals:** Animals can easily communicate with each other with no need for linguistic systems. Instead they point, gesture, smell, and touch one another, just as humans do. It shouldn't be very surprising then that certain standing positions taken by us send certain ranking order socially and are comparable to the gesture of our primate relatives. Yawning, which many consider a signal of being bored, is something that even fish do. In addition to this, the manner in which we shake hands, smile, and hold objects in our hands can all be read into and interpreted to show mental states.

- **Emotional Undertones:** Nonverbal signals are very much related to feelings. It's pretty simple to recognize which emotions are beneath particular facial expressions, and we do this naturally. Certain emotions seem to be universal and innate, like disgust, happiness, and fear. We are able to show feelings and emotion using touch, too. At certain times, a hug can say more than spoken words can. In addition to this, not everyone is great at sharing their feelings verbally, which explains the popularity and prevalence of avenues such as counseling and role playing.

- **Beneficial Silent Signals:** At times, the signs and signals of nonverbal communication work efficiently and smoothly, without those involved having to think much about what is happening. One person sends a gesture or signal and the other person receives it, both knowing intuitively what the unspoken gesture was meant to convey. For instance, if people are speaking in a group and one person raises up their hand, the speaker will likely pause to see what that person is asking instinctively. In this way, silent signals can be highly beneficial for all involved.

- **Interpreting Signals:** Other times, the person sending the signal is not aware that they are doing so. They might be fidgeting with their shirt, tapping their foot, glancing around, and more. The person observing this could notice and interpret the visual information without the sender knowing that they have conveyed anything. The receiver of the signals can benefit from this information in certain situations, if they correctly interpret the information.

- **Deliberate Influence:** Some people might intentionally send messages to others by stepping into their personal space, mimicking their movements, or by lightly touching them. Caught up in the words being spoken, the receiver might be unaware of what the sender is trying to do with their deliberate yet subtle actions. Using subtle cues like this to influence people is a powerful method of persuasion. Since the conscious thought and attention of the receiver of information is not involved, they can't reject what is being proposed. Successful marketing and political influence makes use of this method of persuasion on a regular basis.

That being said, often times all people involved in a social situation are unaware of what is communicated or signaled. For example a person sending nonverbal cues might display certain pheromones signaling sexual interest, or have dilated pupils signaling the same, without either party being aware that this is happening. This can then result in unexplained and instant attraction between them.

Be Careful with Assumptions about Body Language

There are a lot of common tips out there to reading people's body language, such as someone playing with their wedding ring while talking to an attractive stranger and the assumption that they wish to take it off. Or someone who crosses their legs a lot being sexually repressed. There is a big temptation in the field of body language to try to read a lot into these motions and try to interpret some type of unconscious message being sent, rather than looking to a simpler or more obvious explanation. For people becoming interested in this subject, it's always a good idea to remember that it's possible to read people wrong.

Not every instance of someone crossing their arms signifies that they are uncertain or insecure. Perhaps the room is just cold or they are sitting in chair without armrests. People communicate nonverbal messages often without realizing it, but this shouldn't lead observers to assume that every gesture has an unconscious or unfulfilled need at its base. Sometimes, gestures are just gestures. People internalize and acquire gestures or even facial expressions from teachers, parents, or their favorite actors. While some body language cues signify hidden urges, hopes, or desires, most probably do not.

Remember that Words Matter, too

It's a myth that body language is always a stronger indicator of someone's true thoughts or feelings than their words. People who research body language and nonverbal communication have a tendency to rely on it too much or believe that it is the "end all be all" of communication. Of course it's important and powerful, but words are very apt as well.

- ***Professional Situations:*** *Think about how successful poetry is at getting messages across, or how important it is for politicians to be articulate and well-spoken. Only the ones who have the best skills in verbal charm and charisma can succeed in those areas. This is proof that words and verbal communication are highly important to the way we live and function as human beings in the world.*

- ***Fewer Options:*** *In addition to this, one using gestures for communication without words will make it immediately obvious that there are far fewer options for getting a message across than there are with words. This is why we have the capabilities of both speech, and reading and sending body language signals. One is incomplete without the other. Although it's possible to communicate using only one, it doesn't always provide a full picture. This is like comparing talking to someone on the phone with actually sitting next to them.*

Differing Degrees of Body Language Cues

What makes communication in body language so powerful is that it indicates an individual's mental or emotional state due to nervous system changes. Of course, when an extreme feeling is being felt, such as anger, it is going to show through even if someone is trying to hide it. In addition to this, feelings like sexual arousal are difficult to keep hidden, along with guilt. But these states are almost always proof of extreme feeling states, not typical or everyday states. At times, body language is loud and unavoidable, while at other times, it's the subtlest of signals.

Trying to Control Emotions makes them more Obvious

Part of learning how to read and analyze people means understanding the way emotions work for yourself. Many times, when you attempt to hide your own feelings, this only makes them more apparent to those around you.

- **Some are Uncontrollable:** Some body language cues, like touch and gestures, are easy to control, but others like the dilation of your pupils and sweating, are involuntary. Many times, people try to hide their true motives or anxiety, but can't due to the physiological evidence of them. This is especially difficult or, in some cases, completely impossible, to hide if you don't know anything about body language. This is yet another good reason to be learning about the subject.

- **A Lack of Awareness:** *The average person, while engaged in a conversation, is not aware of what their feet or legs are doing, but could control this if they became aware. In addition to this, most people are not consciously reading the nonverbal cues of other people, such as the tiny facial expressions people show when speaking or the subtle posture changes that indicate a shift in mood. Although we don't think about this in a straightforward way, parts of us still notice most of the time and respond to it instantly with our instincts.*

- **Reading Cues in Retrospect:** *As soon as certain behaviors are apparent on video, they are surprisingly easy to understand and decipher. As soon as a person becomes aware of how they are acting and what signals they are sending, reading other people's cues becomes much easier. To put it in another way, to understand yourself makes it easier to understand those around you. In addition, hindsight can be a useful way to get better at reading body language cues and nonverbal signals.*

Of course, some individuals will try to keep their nonverbal cues under control at all times. This could be for many reasons, such as hiding true motives, or having a profession as an actor. But for the most part, the more you attempt to hide or control what you're feeling (especially when it's a strong emotion), the more obvious it will become in your facial expressions, gestures, and body posture. Also, once you get good at reading body language, no one can really hide theirs from you. Even the best actor in the world has to let their mask slip sometimes.

Simple Techniques to Start with

Learning how to read people is an art form, and it involves tapping into sense that we might not usually use. Part of being a human is reading unspoken cues given to us by the people around us. This helps us not only to decipher how they feel and what they think, but what they are like on a deeper level than the surface. Most people who wish to learn how to interpret nonverbal and verbal signals have a hope to see to the core of other people instead of just the everyday masks most people put forth. Logic is not enough to help you figure out a person's entire story, or even all of what they feel at this very moment. You have to tap into other important sources of data and information so you can figure out how to read intuitive signals that everyone is constantly giving off.

Looking Past Biases to Analyze People

To read people, you need to know how to surrender your biases, preconceived ideas, ego clashes, resentments, and any baggage you have that could be clouding your judgment and preventing you from accurately reading someone. The ideal here is to stay objective and observe data without twisting it in your mind to fit your prejudices or biases. This is no easy task. Whether your hope is to read your partner, co-worker, or even your boss, in order to read people, you have to break down some walls within yourself. Although our intellectual minds are undeniably brilliant and advanced, they can limit us. Those who are good at reading others accurately have trained themselves to see what isn't obvious to the rest of us. They have accessed advanced senses in order to access valuable and intuitive information and insight.

Observing Physical, Nonverbal Clues

Studies have shown us that words only communicate a portion of what we are really saying, while other cues communicate the rest. In this area, although it may sound counterintuitive, the idea is to let go of thinking about trying to read nonverbal signals. Getting too analytical or intense about it will only hinder your progress. Remember to stay calm, comfortable, and just observe and perceive. As humans, we are like other animals in that we can instinctively read each other. Most of the time, it's a matter of getting out of our own way in order to make this happen.

- **Appearance does Matter:** Appearance is something to pay attention to when it comes to trying to read people. As you attempt to observe them, notice if they are dressed up in nice, business-themed clothes that shout ambition or a t-shirt and jeans combo that appear to signal rest and relaxation. Are they wearing a necklace with a large religious symbol on it, or perhaps a revealing outfit? All of this can tell you what this person's motives are.

- **Pay Attention to Posture:** *When you are observing a person's posture, notice whether they appear confident with their head held up, or whether they appear to cower as they walk. Do they stick out their chest as a signal of dominance, or try to walk by unnoticed? A person's posture says a lot about them, even if it's only about their mood at that particular moment.*

- **Physical Indicators and Movements:** *The direction a person leans in can be very telling; for instance, someone who leans toward you likes you, and someone who leans away from someone typically doesn't feel very favorably about them. Another common sign is the crossing of the legs or arms. When someone does this, it can signal that they are feeling defensive or angry. Keep in mind that this isn't a foolproof sign, and that someone might just be cold.*

  If someone appears to be trying to hide their hands, in their pockets for example, it may indicate that they are attempting to hide something or feel uncomfortable. On a similar note, someone who is biting their lips or picking at their nails, this could indicate anxiety, feeling pressured, or feeling awkward. In addition to this, someone pursing their lips could mean that they feel bitter or angry, while clenched teeth signal tension or frustration.

It's possible to interpret a person's inner-state beyond what they are saying using your intuition, which relies on gut feelings and instinct rather than just logic. It's unspoken data that we receive through images, sudden moments of insight, and bodily perceptions, instead of analytic logical reasoning. If you hope to gain understanding of a person, what matters is who they are deep down, not superficial aspects of them. Tapping into your intuition can help you look beyond the obvious to get a fuller picture. Here are some intuitive clues to look out for when reading people:

- **Noticing Gut Feelings:** Pay attention to what your gut is telling you, particularly when you are very first meeting someone, which gives you a reaction based on pure instinct before your mind chimes in. This can show you whether you feel comfortable or not. These reactions happen instantly and tell you whether or not you can trust someone. These reactions evolved with us for a reason, so make sure you honor them and pay attention.

- **Spontaneous Insights**: Pay special attention to sudden flashes of information or insight that come to you about someone. If you are like the average person, you have a constant stream of thoughts flowing through your mind, which makes it easy to lose important data that could be useful to you. Make it a point to notice these things.

- **Noticing Empathy:** *If you are a particularly sensitive person, you should be able to feel other people's moods empathetically or intuitively. When you interact with someone who is very joyful, you feel it intensely as though it's your joy, and the same goes for negative emotions. This can be an accurate gauge for what another person is feeling, depending on your own personality.*

Sensing the Emotions of Others

Emotions make up the impressions we give to other people, which are then registered in an intuitive way. Some people are easy and nice to spend time around, while others feel draining and make you want to run away. Reading and analyzing people has a lot to do with learning how to consciously sense this. Here are some key tips for doing just that:

- **Pay Attention to Eyes:** *It's no secret that eyes are very expressive and revealing. Take some time to start observing the people around you and their eyes. Do they appear to be frustrated, interested, and intelligent? Do they appear to be uncomfortable or anxious? Another very useful part of the face to look at is the eyebrows. Are the person's eyebrows pointing upward or downward? This can tell a lot about the mood they are in and whether or not they are listening.*

- **Pay Attention to Physical Touch:** *Another way to start accurately reading people is to pay attention to physical touch* such as a hug or a handshake. Next time you encounter this with someone, notice whether it feels inviting and warm, or cold and calculating. Does the hug feel confident and comfortable, or nervous and stand-offish? These can tell you a lot about the person's inner-state.

- **Laugh and Voice**: The volume and tone of voice a person uses says a lot about what they are feeling. When a person talks a lot and has a boisterous laugh, it's safe to assume that they are quite confident. When a person who usually sounds this way sounds very different, it's an indication that they are feeling something else. For someone who is usually really quiet and withdrawn who is being louder, something is obviously up with them. These are all the types of clues you need to be watching for in order to learn how to read body language effectively and accurately.

All of this information is useful for reading people, along with other indicators such as how well you know them, whether or not they are comfortable with you, and the context and situation you find yourself in. Someone who is very happy and boisterous at a concert, obviously, is not always naturally that way, and it's likely just the situation making them feel that way. Someone who appears sad at a party might be a naturally sullen person or they might just be having a bad day. Take all of this into consideration before you jump to conclusions about people and their body language. Over time, you will get better at reading it accurately.

Before Trying to Analyze Someone

Base lining is likely the most crucial yet misunderstood aspects of interpreting nonverbal communication signals. This refers to a person's normal actions or motions in terms of gestures, tone of voice, and more. This is important because it's not realistic to expect to be able to read a person without knowing what to look for as far as abnormal or unusual behaviors go. For instance, to try to interpret someone's body language that is usually moving a lot as bothered would be incorrect, since that is not outside of their typical behaviors. A person's specific nuances and personality quirks make up who they are and the way they act, and everyone has a group of cues that are normal according to the way they usually act.

Looking for Out of Character Responses

If a person is high strung naturally, it could be a bit difficult to tell when they are upset, agitated, or anxious about something. But if someone who is usually hyperactive and moving around a lot suddenly freezes in the face of a new situation, this could be a signal that they are feeling something strongly that can be read and interpreted in their body language. Deviating from their norm is not a signal that something specific is going on, only that something is going on. As the person who wishes to read or analyze the other, it's up to you to

determine what has changed in the environment and what they are
likely feeling due to context and the situation at hand.

Base Lining and What to Look for

- **How someone Sits:** Cues can be found in a variety of signals
  that people show as far as what their baseline is. For
  example, the way they typically sit.

- **Hand Gestures:** How does the person usually gesture with
  their hands? When they are resting, are their hands fidgeting
  around and moving a lot or simply clasped in their lap?

- **Legs and Feet:** Next, you should pay attention to their feet
  and legs. When they are standing up, what are they doing
  with their feet? Do they have their legs crossed usually?
  Perhaps they are tapping their feet as though they are
  anxious most of the time.

- **Standing Posture and Walking:** How does a person stand
  when they are at rest? How does their posture shift and
  change as they walk?

Any and all of the above clues can tell you how a person normally is
when they are simply comfortable or relaxed. This is how you can tell

when they begin to act in a way that is not typical to them, and then move on to figuring out why and what it means.

Catching Subtle or Abrupt Changes

The next step lies in making sure you notice when a person's normal behavior changes or shifts. If you don't stay aware of subtle changes, you are missing your chance to catch the clues that will help you read someone's nonverbal messages.

- ***An Example of a Clue:*** *If you see a kid who is very happy and exuberant, acting animated and joyful, who suddenly starts to withdraw into himself and become quiet right as his big brother enters the room, this can indicate what is going on with them at the moment. Nonverbal cues and body language are linked directly to our deepest emotions, so when you notice a shift in those cues, something has caused it to come about, and it's usually whatever happened right before the change.*

- ***Touchy Topics:*** *Changes in a person's body language are not just about specific events. Instead, they might be related to topics or certain words spoken. For example, there might be two married partners talking to each other and laughing together, but once an ex of one of them is brought up in conversation, the entire mood might change. This doesn't necessarily mean that the comment was harmful or threatening; even a casual remark can produce an abrupt* change in mood if it has strong emotion tied to it. For example, the husband may start to appear angry and closed off right as the name of the ex comes into conversation.

To someone observing this happen, it becomes obvious that that person is a sore issue in the marriage and the abrupt change in the vibe between the couple, from positive to negative, shows that the specific topic is the culprit. It's up to you as the observer and analyzer to notice what it was that caused this change, so that you can correctly assess what the person you're observing is feeling or thinking.

Investigators of criminal matters typically steer the suspects they are talking to away from the topic by bringing up unrelated topics like hobbies or past times. This allows the investigator to accurately read how the person looks when they are relaxed. As soon as they have established that person's baseline behaviors, they can start to bring up facts about their investigation in order to see how the suspect responds to the words. For example, they may start talking about items that have nothing to do with the trail, and then switch suddenly to an incriminating weapon to see if the suspect begins displaying signs of nervousness or guilt.

Not Objective in all Cases, but Helpful

When it comes to investigations of criminal events, a piece of evidence such as the weapon used for murder is often kept secret from all but the investigators themselves. This means that only someone guilty should show visceral emotions as a result of seeing it. Although interrogations like this don't always lead to the guilty being found and convicted, it can give valuable signals and clues for which direction to take. Similar to all body language, these signs can tell us whether or not we are heading the right way in our suspicions.

- **Learning to see More:** People who are not used to looking for the baselines of others will find it hard to accurately assess others who aren't similar to them. This is because their main reference for what is normal is their own selves or those who they typically associate with. They will then be unable to see the habits, cultures, and characteristics of those outside of the norm unless they practice.

- **Practice on those you Know:** You can begin to hone your skills of getting baselines by observing those around you; family, instructors, friends, colleagues, and more. Anyone you talk with on a regular basis, or even those you don't, should be observed. Not only will this make it easier to read them, but you will then have archetypes to use in the future to compare others against. This then enhances your chances of being able to read unfamiliar people instantly in the future.

- **Only one Piece of the Puzzle:** Always remember that getting someone's baseline is only one small part of learning to read their body language. You can't effectively assume that just a simple shift in the way someone is acting means something *objectively, but it can get your attention and cause you to focus on noticing more signs.*

Clarifying Questions about the Change

In a situation where you notice that a change in behavior has happened that deviates from the person's baseline, you should ask some questions to clarify what just happened. Here are some examples to use:

- *Is something wrong with this subject we're talking about?*

- *You seem a bit uncomfortable about this subject, should we talk about it another time?*

- *You seemed to become more passionate and engaged once this topic came up, was it something specific that caused that change?*

Bringing up questions like the one above, and paying close attention to the response they get (of course), can lend you valuable insights into what caused the change in that person. Sometimes, they won't want to talk about it, while other times they will have a simple explanation.

When can you Expect to have a Baseline Established?

You might be understandably wondering how long it typically takes to get a baseline established for a person you're observing. It usually doesn't take very long, since people are giving clues about themselves all the time. It's true that the longer you pay attention to someone, the more accurate your judgments are bound to be, but this isn't always an option. Sometimes, you are thrust into a situation and must act immediately and learn to read these signs quickly. The following guidelines apply to first meeting someone and shaking their hand and also trying to figure out how truthful they are:

- **A Full View:** First, you must make sure that you can fully see the person so you can accurately gauge their feelings, and levels of discomfort and comfort that might come up. If you can, try to walk toward them in an open room with plenty of space to move around. You can reasonably expect that, if you are meeting them for the first time, they will be slightly nervous.

- **A Relaxed Subject:** Ideally, the person you are observing (in this case, the "subject"), should be as relaxed as possible. You can do this by asking them questions about their interests, where they're from, weekend plans, or other small talk topics. Try to build rapport and get them to feel comfortable around you.

- **Asking Questions:** You can then start to ask them questions that are a bit more specific, personal, or emotional. This can let you know, by their responses, how they feel about certain topics. Depending on the situation, you will want to ask about different subjects. For example, if your hope is to gauge whether a person likes you romantically or not, you're going to ask different questions than you would ask if you are interviewing someone for a job.

- **Take Pauses:** Remember to pause after each question you ask. This helps you to not ask too many things at once and overwhelm and stress out the person you're questioning. Allow them enough time to answer and think about what they are saying in order to gain accurate information.

- **Stay Focused:** You should maintain your own personal attention and focus. When someone is stressed out, they will wish to either avoid what you're asking or change the topic altogether. When someone seems eager to change the topic at the first chance, it's a sign they weren't comfortable with what you were discussing.

The More you Listen, the more you Trust

Just because someone is chatting with you a lot, doesn't mean they are being honest and truthful. When you listen to someone talking about any subject, it tends to make you biased about what they are saying. In other words, the more you listen to someone, the more you end up trusting them. Advertisers already know this truth well, and know that the more you hear a message, the more likely you are to believe it, at least on a subconscious level. Over time, when you hear something repeated over and over, part of you begins to accept it as truth.

Nonverbal Signs of Stress

When someone is putting forth a lot of information on a particularly subject, they might seem like a reputable or trustworthy source, even if they aren't in reality. Keep in mind, as you read people, that the amount of data you get from them doesn't matter so much as how accurate what they're saying and expressing is. Here are some key points to keep in mind when you are observing someone who appears to become stressed out:

- **Signals of Stress:** There are a couple of different instances where body language signs of anxiety or discomfort are expressed. The first one will be when you ask a question or some other stimulus comes into play, and the second will be when the person tries to subconsciously soothe themselves through patting their hair or touching their neck.

- **Determine the Cause:** You should next figure out what is causing that person's stressful reaction. Is this happening because they are being asked difficult questions? All body language signals of distress can mean different things, and even honest people can show nervousness at times, so always keep context in mind.

If you have ever wanted to learn how to read people, you should be able to recognize a few key cues for doing this. Being able to effectively interpret these signals and use them to communicate is a necessary foundation for all relationships, personal and professional. However, it isn't just about the words we use to communicate. Body language can say more than words, at times. Again, always keep in mind that the context matters before all else when trying to interpret someone's signals. Someone crossing their arms can, for instance, be a sign that they are angry and defensive, or it could mean something entirely different. Remember the big picture while you observe. It's worth noting that if you start noticing certain signals in others, you can gain a fuller insight by paying attention to your own cues too.

- ***Body Language of the Eyes:*** *A person's eyes don't give a complete picture of what is going on inside of them, but they definitely lend some clues and signals to what they may be thinking or feeling inside. Does the person you're speaking to meet your eyes in a comfortable way and seem okay with looking at you directly as you speak? On the other hand, do they hold extended eye contact? This can either mean sexual interest or an attempt to intimidate you. On the other hand, completely avoiding your eyes shows that someone might feel anxious or nervous.*

  Some people blink faster when they are feeling uncomfortable or stressed out in some way. When it comes to paying attention to people's eyes, you can also follow the direction of their eyes. If someone is staring down at the ground they might feel guilty or simply insecure.

- **Body Language of the Mouth:** Our mouths tell a lot more than just the words that come out of them. If someone seems to be biting their lip a lot, it can be a signal that they are worried or stressed out about something. When someone covers their mouth, it can mean that they are trying to hide something. It's also necessary, while reading body language, to notice the way people smile and whether it's real or fake. Real smiles engage the entire face, particularly the eyes. Fake smiles, on the other hand, only affect the mouth and can be easy to spot once you realize this. In order to figure out whether someone's smile is real or not, look at their eyes.

- **The Nonverbal Cues of the Head:** Our heads hold our brains and most of our organs for sensing, so movements of the head are very expressive and revealing about the way someone is reacting to what they see and sense. If someone has their head upward and pointing forward, they are likely engaged and listening closely to what you're saying in a positive way. Subtle nods and mirrored facial expressions are further proof that this is the case. When someone has their head tilted, it usually means that they are considering your words in an interested way. For someone who is looking down, they might be feeling shameful, defeated, or disapproving of what you're saying.

- **Body Language of the Legs and Arms:** When someone is crossing either their legs, arms, or both, it can signal that they are feeling closed off or in a defensive mood. In addition to this, having their hands hidden behind their back while clasping them, this can show that they are feeling confident. Hands clasped in the front, however, can show that someone is feeling frustrated in certain circumstances. When someone is fidgeting with their feet or hands, this might mean they are irritated or feeling impatient. Always remember, of course, to watch for groups of signals.

- **Posture and Torso Body Language:** Posture is related to the movements of the legs and arms. For example, someone who is crossing their arms might subconsciously be hoping to protect a vulnerable part of their body (the torso). Standing up straight or sitting erect shows that someone is focused and giving their attention to the situation or to what you are saying. This can show that they trust you and feel confident, as well. When someone is slouching forward, it typically shows a lack of energy or that they are trying to block out contact from other people and don't want to be approached. But leaning on something shows that someone is quite comfortable and relaxed with the situation at hand.

Body Language Signals to Recognize

Have you ever wondered what someone is really thinking or feeling? Learning how to analyze people can give you this ability. Quality communication is a must for any healthy relationship and for professional reasons too. Let's look over an important indicator of reading body language.

What Gravity can tell us about Mood

Gravity is actually the most useful tool we have when it comes to reading a person's body language.

- **For Negative Emotions:** Consider this, when someone is feeling downtrodden, sad, or bad in some way, everything about them sort of sags. This includes their face, arms, and even legs. Their head will hang, their shoulders will slouch, and even walking can seem to be difficult to someone in a very bad mood.

- **For Positive Emotions:** On the other side of things, when someone is feeling very positive, gravity appears to be on their side. Their facial muscles move upward, resulting in a

smile, as their arms begin to instinctively reach upward
(picture cheering when your team scores the goal.)

If you want to know how someone is feeling, paying attention to these indicators will give you some clues to their inner state. Another key aspect to understanding this is knowing how to detect when someone is feeling either comfortable or uncomfortable. This is a great way to detect deception or lying. Making sure that someone is relaxed when they are talking to you can help you spot when they deviate from that norm, which relates to the baseline we discussed earlier and will discuss more later. The goal is not to create deceptive body language in someone else, but to notice when it happens.

Detecting Guilty Body Language

- **Signs of Comfort:** *Nonverbal signals that our bodies send subconsciously are the key to detecting when someone is either lying or being truthful. When someone is displaying signs of comfort, they are likely being truthful, because someone who is relaxed doesn't have anything to feel bad about.*

- **Signs of Discomfort:** *When someone feels guilty about something, they are usually carrying around negative and thoughts about themselves everywhere they go. This is because most people are honest naturally and believe that* *they have good hearts and are naturally good people. When someone starts to have bad or guilt-worthy thoughts, on the other hand, feeling comfortable is not easy. You can tell that someone feels guilty about something just by this.*

- ***Being Expressive with Gestures:*** *How expressive a person is with the gestures they use can also be really revealing. For instance, when someone gestures a lot with their arms and hands as they talk, they are likely being truthful. On the other hand, when someone is very restricted or freezes, they might be lying. If someone claims to be telling about something that happened without any gestures, they are probably making up the story. People who are telling the truth want the facts to be straight and don't mind going extra lengths to make that happen.*

How you Affect someone's Body Language

Keep in mind that the way you observe people does have an effect on the way they will act. When someone feels as though they are under observation, they might seem nervous even if they don't have anything to hide or feel guilty about. Looking suspiciously at someone you don't like or intentionally giving them accusatory inquiries will only create an uncomfortable environment for trying to read someone. To make matters confusing, this doesn't necessarily prove that what you did was the cause of their shift in body language.

- **Building Rapport First:** *You have to get someone to feel comfortable and relaxed with you before you can read them in any accurate way. This is done by establishing rapport with them. This can be done by being friendly, subtly mirroring their expressions and tone of voice, and by asking them questions about something that they seem to like or feel passionate about. In essence, building rapport means being nice to someone else. More often than not, this will work in establishing positive relations between you and them.*

- **The Variable:** *When professional scientists conduct experiments or research, what they do is try to keep every factor involved the same, excluding just one factor. This is what is known as the variable, and it refers to what is being specifically measured in the experiment. To put it another way, it's what they are trying to test reactions to. This variable is what is trying to be changed as the experiment is conducted. When you are trying to figure someone out and read them, try to have calm conditions so that one variable will stand out.*

- **Staying Neutral:** *In addition to building rapport, staying neutral is the best way to accurately gauge a person's body language. If you seem too obsessed or eager to analyze them, it won't give you an accurate reading of who they are, because they might sense this. Therefore, when you hope to read someone and uncover their true feelings, you should try to stay as calm and neutral as possible, only asking questions* and observing them in order to uncover variables in their behavior. The more neutral you seem, the more comfortable they will feel with acting like themselves around you.

How the Nose relates to Body Language

This may sound confusing at first. After all, how can the nose show anything about how someone is feeling? Well, when someone is feeling stressed out, their skin becomes flushed with blood. When these areas are flushed, they become more sensitive, and our hands are naturally drawn there. This means that we can notice when someone is uncomfortable by paying attention to these signals. When the capillaries in the nose become enlarged, our hands might subconsciously go there in an attempt to soothe that feeling. Touching one's nose can also signal that they are lying or uncomfortable.

It's usually just a very fast touch on the side, but at times it could be more persistent than that. When someone touches their face, it can either mean that they are scratching an actual itch, or that they are simply stressed out and uncomfortable. Touching the face because of an emotion is done in order to try to fix the feeling, instead of due to a physical feeling and need.

What does it Take to Appear Trustworthy

To come across as more trustworthy to other people, you should eliminate or reduce face touching. This will make you seem more natural and at ease, or at least appear consistent in different situations and scenarios. Someone who has a genuine itch will usually scratch their nose in a situation that doesn't seem suspicious, such as sitting and not talking with anyone or talking about something unimportant. On the other hand, someone who touches their noise while describing something significant should be watched closely for further signs of deception.

Being Unenthusiastic and Uncommitted

When someone is telling the truth, they will often go the extra mile to commit to what they are saying and show enthusiasm. While a liar might begin this way, it doesn't stick and they usually end up trailing off or appearing to lose gusto as they go. Liars often are not committed to the lies they tell. Since they don't have anything real invested in what they are lying about, they aren't as enthusiastic in what they say and claim. To put it another way, the mind of a deceptive person does not let them show enthusiasm often. Instead of vehemently claiming that they are innocent, they are usually much duller in their responses to accusations.

When we were kids and we saw something scary, our immediate instinct was to block our eyes. This is something that sticks around with us, although it may change form as we grow older. For instance, instead of actually covering their eyes for an extended about of time, an adult may simply squint lightly as a subtle way to block what they are seeing.

- **Eye Covering:** Another related behavior for body language is literally blocking the eyes with something, like the hands for example. Someone might cover their eyes briefly if they don't approve of what they are seeing. For instance, someone afraid of horror films may cover their eyes when a preview for one comes on the television. In addition, someone might rub their eyes briefly when someone is doing something they don't approve of.

- **Pupil Dilation and Constriction:** The size of our pupils can also tell a lot about our state of mind. Whenever we approve of what we are seeing, our pupils open up and dilate in order to allow more light in. On the other hand though, when we are looking at something we don't approve of, they will constrict. This effect also happens when someone is squinting or constricting their eyelids since these functions are meant to keep less light from touching the eyes. This action brings what the person is seeing into a smaller and tighter frame of focus, which evolutionarily should have protected us from a threat or attack.

Squinting the eyes to focus better can be seen in people who try to read when they aren't wearing glasses and don't have great vision. In addition, this effect is created by trying to read through a paper with a tiny hole in it.

Keeping a Notebook for your Observations

Keeping a body language notebook can be a great way to keep track of what you notice in others, as well as to look back on to see how accurate your assessments were. Here are the steps for doing that:

- **Decide what to Focus on:** At the beginning of each day, write at least one paragraph about what you will be focusing on in your goals to get better at analyzing people. This can be noticing people's tones of voice, their facial expressions, or their posture. At first, you should try to focus on only one at a time.

- **Think on this throughout the Day:** The next step is to consider what you wrote about throughout your day; paying attention to everyone you come into contact with, including your boss, the cashier, or your friends. What are their postures saying? What are their faces saying? Pay attention to whatever it is you decided to focus on for that day, and keep notes in your notebook if you can.

- **Decide what the Signals Mean:** *Next, try to determine what the signals that you witnessed in people (for example a slouching posture or a drooped eyebrow) meant. Was that person feeling sad? Did that person's bouncing walking posture make it seem as though something great had just happened to them? Ideally, you should try to make guesses about people and situations that you can confirm later. For instance, if you can try to gauge the mood of your friends or family, you can then ask them later if your suspicions were correct. With strangers, this isn't as possible, but that doesn't mean you shouldn't still try to read them for practice.*

- **Record your Thoughts at the end of the Day:** *Next, try to write at least another paragraph in your body language journal at night before you go to bed. Reflect on what your goal was for that day in noticing people and whether or not you learned anything about reading people. If you were right about something, write that down. If you were wrong about your suspicions of what someone's nonverbal cues meant, write that down too. All of this information can help you to becoming an expert at reading people.*

- **Use the Information:** *Now, the entire purpose of the journal; to read people. When you notice groups of hints that someone is thinking or feeling a certain way and then can later confirm that you were right, this is a sign you're getting better at reading people. Make sure that you are writing all of this down so that you can use this information.*

With time, if you focus on it, you will learn how to read people accurately. Of course, it is not possible to always be right, but it's possible to be right most of the time. Keeping a body language journal is a great way to improve your practices at getting better with it.

Getting a Body Language Reading Buddy

It's always helpful to have a friend to practice something with. If you have a friend who is also interested in psychology or learning to read people, you should discuss this subject together and make it a point to practice reading people together. This can mean simple people watching or just having conversations about what you think that someone was thinking or feeling at the party you two just attended.

Knowing When Someone Likes You

One difficult, complex, and at times even frustrating aspects of relationships and dating is attempting to know for sure whether they are feeling romantic towards you or not. Many people have looked for advice in the realm of whether a man or woman finds you appealing, how to know what they want, and more. In attempting to analyze a person's feelings and thoughts like this, though, it's easy to make mistakes based on misconceptions. For instance, because of your personal biases and inclinations, you might assume that someone is not interested even when they definitely are, or on the other hand optimistically see that someone is interested when they really are not.

In both of the cases listed above, biases concerning misreading people can either cause you to miss opportunities or make a fool of yourself. In addition to this, perceptions that are wrong in these areas might lead to someone being seen as "just a friend" when there could have been something more, or an arrangement that pleases neither party. These biases can also lead to difficulties and complications in platonic relationships. Considering all of this, why can it be so difficult to read signals correctly as to whether the person likes you or not? What can you do to get better at this? After all, someone who wishes to learn to analyze and read body language better probably has this ability high on their list of priorities and skills. First, let's focus on this concept strictly as it applies to dating. Later, we'll move onto other types of relationships and situations.

Perception and Managing Errors

In social and evolutionary psychology, the subject of reading people's minds in romantic situations and relationships has been discussed in something known as the theory of error management. This concept states that people are very biased in their perceptions, as far as romance goes, since we have developed and evolved this way in order to serve other benefits for mating and furthering the species. To be more specific, this concept relies on the idea that the costs of mating are different, on a biological level, for males and females.

- **Men and Women:** For a guy to contribute sperm, it isn't very costly. For a woman to become pregnant, on the other hand, takes a lot of energy and costs quite a bit of time and more. This results in guys having evolved not to miss easy opportunities for sex, and have biases that have evolved to see desire in females even where there is none. But women have evolved to avoid guys who don't wish to invest in them and appear to have evolved to discount certain committed signals, regardless of how sincere the man may be. Obviously, this can lead to issues when a guy falsely assumes interest from a woman, or when the woman misses out on a great opportunity with a guy due to being too skeptical of his intentions.

- **Projection:** A few different studies have been done on this topic in order to take a closer look at these concepts and ideas. They found support for men's tendencies to believe that there is more sexual interest than there really is, and the tendency of females to be overly skeptical even when there is no need. These studies also suggested that other biases can play a role in this arena, as well. Men might, for example, project the interest in commitment or sex that they feel onto the women, and vice versa. Considering all of that, it's no wonder this subject is so complicated and, at times, hard to figure out! Overall, we might not be as accurate as we believe in reading each other's signals for purely evolutionary and biological reasons.

Figuring out if Someone really Likes you

Considering the previous information, how are you supposed to be able to know when someone is showing real signals that they like you? How are you supposed to get past the inherent biases that might be clouding your judgment? The solution here relies on the idea that not everyone is wrong all the time. Whenever you do get it right, it's typically because you have relied on logical, objective interest indicators, instead of biased perceptions and feelings you had about the person and situation. To clarify, this means that your accuracy is more likely when you pay attention to real signals the other person is sending, and not your own feelings and personal ideas and wishes. This means that in order to gain a clearer understanding of someone's romantic or sexual interest in you, pay attention to what they are doing as well as what they are saying, not how you're feeling.

So, what exactly should you be noticing in order to figure this out? When you're trying to gauge someone's interest, especially if it's someone you feel very attracted to, it's difficult to know what to focus on. Start with these indicators:

- ***Nonverbal Cues:*** *If a person is actually interested, they will usually be displaying forward and open nonverbal cues and body language. Even if they take a few moments to get warmed up to you, if they like you they will probably start to lean toward you and become animated as they talk and gesture. In addition, they will probably make eye contact (with exceptions for shy people, of course). In essence, when someone likes you, they display positive behavior toward you and tend to focus on you fully.*

- ***Physical Touch:*** *The next behavior that can lend you a clue about attraction and interest from someone is physical touch. If someone is interested and attracted, they are most likely going to figure out some way to start touching you more often, along with being receptive to you physically touching them. That might start with innocent handshakes and progress into embraces, or more. When you want to know for sure what they desire, you can check to see how they kiss, if the situation is appropriate.*

- **Commitment and Personal Investment**: When a person is really interested and in love, they are committed to having a relationship with you, and will make it known to others, telling their family and friends, and including you in different aspects of their daily life. In addition to this, they'll attempt to gain your investment and commitment by paying attention to your needs, looking nice, and more. Essentially, when someone is really committed and invested, they will be proud of you and supportive of who you are.

- **Grateful Attitudes:** Lately, when someone cares about you on a deep level, they don't hesitate to show that they are grateful when you do nice things for them. This could be taking care of your needs, bringing you thoughtful objects or gifts, cooking you dinner, or doing favors for you in other areas. When they care, they say thank you in a way that lets you know that they truly mean it. To put it simply, when someone really cares, they will make sure you know that they appreciate you.

While paying attention to the cues and signals above, you should have a much clearer idea when someone likes you and wants to get involved with you in a way that goes beyond friendship. This can also help you to know when someone just wants something platonic, or perhaps just physical and nothing emotional. No one enjoys simply wondering without knowing for sure, so now you have the necessary tools to find out for yourself instead of being confused.

Gauging someone's General Interest or Favor in you

Who hasn't wanted to be able to tell when people like them, either in a romantic way or simply a friendly way? Have you ever wondered whether someone you have an attraction for returns those feelings? Do you want to know whether your coworkers or boss respects you? There is actually a simple method for finding this out. In order to sum it up and get your answer, try to get the person to laugh. If you notice that they laugh easily, they probably like you. When the opposite is true, they probably do not.

- **How this Applies to the Dating World:** *Many people have dedicated hours, days, and weeks of their lives to learning how to date and meet people. Along the way, some will have noticed that when someone is laughing at another person's jokes, it's a sign that they feel favorably about them. One only has to observe a man trying to chat up a woman who is not laughing or smiling at all to know what the answer will be if he tries to ask her out on a date. Where else is this knowledge useful and handy?*

- **How this Knowledge relates to Professional Life:** *A lot can be said about how this applies to the job world. For example, perhaps you've worked a job with a boss you didn't really like. Even if you never told them that outright, perhaps they subconsciously would have noticed it from the fact that you didn't laugh when they told jokes. Who do you think would receive more favor from the boss, the person who never* *laughs, or the employees who always do? This is an example of this psychological dynamic at play.*

- **Testing Social Conditions:** *Humor is something that might have evolved alongside humans as a method for indicating important interests, either between family members, allies, friends, or potential mates. In other words, people might initiate jokes or humor in order to test reactions of people and figure out where they stand with them on a social level. People are going to be more interesting to us if they respond to our humor, and us to them when we respond to theirs. Whether or not the people involved are actually funny, people are more likely to respond favorably to someone's humor if they already like and appreciate them. On a similar note, even if you're a comedic genius, someone won't laugh at your jokes if they don't like you.*

A Method for Feeling out New People

Whenever someone meets someone new, it's a process to find out whether or not there's any type of desirable relationship or dynamic they can have with them. By attempting to strike up a humorous interaction, you can indicate which direction your interest or lack of interest might be taking. This can be determined within a few short minutes of meeting someone, typically, but in some cases it could take longer. When you have the time to get to know someone through repeated visits, and there's no reason to hurry along finding out how they feel, the indications listed in the previous chapter should be appropriate and sufficient. However, situations vary a lot from person to person, so here are some more guidelines.

Testing out People you Already Know using Humor

With strangers, figuring out how someone feels can be compared to doing a puzzle in a dark room. Where are you to start if you have no idea how someone usually is? You might find it easier to start out with friends, or to test reactions with people who you already are familiar with. That way, you are already aware of how they feel for you and whether your assumptions are right or wrong. On a similar note, for people who already know each other quite well, humor can be used to test out the way the relationship is faring.

- **Testing Satisfaction:** *Humorous interactions between people who are already in a relationship or friends can help both people decide whether they are in alignment with each other or truly satisfied with how things are going. Someone may, for example, notice that their significant other doesn't laugh at their jokes anymore and intuitively recognize this as a signal that the relationship is headed south. It may only become clear in retrospect that around the time this starts to happen, the relationship begins to crumble. Learning to recognize this is important because it can offer valuable signs of when something needs to be fixed before the relationship is ruined.*

- **Testing Making up from a Fight:** *Humor can also be used between friends, relatives, or romantic partners for testing* *the grounds after a fight has happened. Consider this, a person is not likely to laugh at your attempts at humor if any ill feelings remain. If they do respond and laugh at your attempts, it indicates that they are at least open to resolving the issues and moving forward.*

Humor has many functions in life. However, this theory states that the most important function it serves is to prove the existence or nonexistence of interest in regards to social relations, whether that be enemies, friends, or partners. It's also useful in professional situations and settings. When someone doesn't laugh at your jokes, it can feel like the ultimate rejection and signal that something isn't right between you. So, start noticing who around you can always make you laugh, as well as the people who are always laughing at your jokes.

How to Tell When Someone is Lying

Humans can tell when someone is lying only about half the time, or roughly 54 percent of the time. To get better at being able to spot liars and prevent yourself from being fooled by deceitful people, it's important to understand the science behind detecting lies in other people. The science of lie detection has existed and been a fascination for countless years and it's quite understandable why that is. Who wouldn't want to know, for example, whether their boss really approves of their performance or not? How about whether your friend is telling you the truth about the draft you just showed them of your first ever novel?

Deception to Protect Social Order

As mentioned before, some measure of deception is necessary to help our society function. It isn't always something bad, as some people mistakenly believe. In fact, it can be helpful and a great tool for navigating the world, in some situations. There are a few different ways that all of us lie in our everyday lives that help things function smoothly, preventing confrontation. Here are some examples of that:

- **Professional Situations:** Professional customer service people, or politicians for that matter, often have to feign a façade of being very friendly or relatable in order to make their jobs run smoother and easier. If a sales person, for example, tells a client that they hate their job and don't want to be there, it's probably not going to go so well.

- **Everyday Politeness:** The social norms we have in place have been put there for a reason. When you shop at a store or accidentally bump someone on the bus, it's polite to respond in a friendly manner. This makes certain experiences more pleasant and bearable for all of us. Even if acting like you don't care (when that's how you really feel) would be more honest technically, it isn't always the best response.

- **To Protect Feelings:** Sometimes, it's favorable to tell "white lies" to protect the feelings of other people. For instance, if a kid comes up to you and asks if their painting is great, and it looks like one big shapeless blob, is it better to tell the truth or to stretch the truth a bit?

Now these are all situations of basically harmless deception that most agree are acceptable and even preferable, at times. There are other situations, especially those involving personal relationships, on the other hand, where deception can be a very bad thing. Part of being able to be close to others is being able to trust what they say, so let's look more into the concept of lying.

Quick Facts about Dishonesty

If anyone desires to understand people or learn to read them accurately and correctly, knowing about dishonesty will only help you. Here are some key points and interesting facts to keep in mind and consider regarding this subject:

- **The Signs:** People who are skilled at learning how to spot lies focus on signs such as tone of voice, body language, facial expressions, and analysis of spoken statements in order to determine deception. This is similar to a polygraph in that the person is being trained to recognize nerves, guilt, and hidden feelings the way the polygraph would measure sweat, respiration and heart rates.

- **The Benefit of Learning:** Studies have proven that taking the time to learn techniques for detecting lies can improve your ability to spot lies up to 90 percent.

- **Statistics about Lying:** Studies show that extroverts are more prone to deception than introverts are, and that males are more likely to lie than females. Over 80 percent of all lies will pass by undetected.

The Learned Habit of Deception

The positive news about lying is that it's a learned habit, meaning that it can be unlearned. In order to test the fact that lying is something learned, researchers conducted a study involving a group of kids aged three years old alone and asked them not to look across the room at a concealed toy. Nearly all of them looked anyway, but when they were asked about looking, only 38 percent of them told the truth about breaking the rule. When this same experiment was done with a group of kids aged five years, not a single one admitted that they looked. This led researchers to conclude that children who were older had already learned, even at five, that trouble often followed being honest, and that lying is better in some cases.

The Basics of Lie Detection

Spotting lies is all about trying to go back to the basics; the truth. The way humans learn how to spot lies isn't so you can judge others or feel better than them. This is all about equipping you with the principles you need to have truthful and honest relationships and interactions with people, and improved communication with them. The science of lie detection is quite complex, as any psychological subject is. So here are the basics to get you started.

- **Gauging Normal Behaviors:** The most crucial step to learning how to spot lies in other people is establishing a baseline. We discussed this in chapter three, but it's a bit of a different process for lie detection. As mentioned before, a person's baseline is the way they act in typical, everyday situations. In other words, it's the way they look and act when they are being honest and truthful. When you are hoping to decipher a person's feelings and tell when they are being untruthful, you first have to realize the way they act when they aren't.

This can be done by talking about general and neutral topics, which is easy in situations like first meeting someone at a social gathering or in a meeting. Begin with some questions that are non-threatening and wouldn't require any deception, like weather-related topics or weekend plans. Whatever would count as "small talk" should work well for this step. As they are answering, notice how their body is positioned, the way their voice sounds, and the movements they make such as fidgeting. Imagine recording a sort of mental video of this.

- **Noticing Changes:** *This next step involves noticing that the baseline behavior of the person you're paying attention to has shifted in some way. Similar to the way a polygraph senses sweat or heart rate spikes, you also can notice a fidgeting foot or sudden facial movements that weren't there a moment ago. Now, it's important to note that there's no objective signal that a person is definitely lying, which is why a baseline is necessary. Each time a person deviates from this norm, it's a signal you should pay attention to.*

Physical Clues that someone is being Deceptive

Red flags might also come up when you notice a clue that someone is being deceptive in their physical actions. Studies show that there are over 30 signals that can mean someone is telling a lie. In this section, we will cover a couple of those cues.

- **Nodding the Opposite Way:** *Oftentimes, when someone lies, simple body movements can indicate this, such as nodding. Someone lying might, for instance, say "no" while nodding without realizing that they are doing it, revealing their subconscious feelings.*

- **Lifting one Shoulder Slightly:** *Studies show that people will lift one shoulder slightly, oftentimes, if they are being deceptive. This is believed to be because they are subconsciously shrugging due to not believing their own words.*

Noticing Groups of Red Flags

When you notice a single deviation from the person's baseline behavior, it's not enough evidence to assume that they are being deceptive with you. The best way to go about this is to notice when there are at least three signs in a single response. This is known as a group of red flags. If you notice a group of strange behaviors or shifts in the person's baseline behavior, then you have either caught them in a lie or have started talking about a topic that is uncomfortable for them. Depending on the situation and how well you know them, either of these scenarios could warrant further discussion or investigation as the conversation progresses.

Limited Movements in Liars

Someone who is lying usually doesn't gesture very much, and if they do, it isn't with very much enthusiasm, as we briefly mentioned earlier. They might instead start a story and then weakly trail off, ending lamely without finishing their thoughts or stories in a strong way.

- *__Not Moving Much:__ They might also subconsciously limit the motions of their hands and arms by locking them in place or by tightly clasping them in a seemingly strained way. White knuckles are one indication of this, as is a lack of much natural movement in the person.*

- *__Hidden Hands:__ Liars might hide their hands somewhere that they won't be visible and give them away due to fidgeting or restless movements. They might hide them underneath a table or inside of their jacket pockets.*

- *__A Locked Body:__ When someone appears to have reduced movement in their entire body, this could be a sign of deception and discomfort. Their whole body, including the torso, feet, arms, and head, might appear to be locked. Someone who is honesty will give energy toward gesturing and making sure that people believe what they are saying. They don't mind doing extra work to make sure that their point gets across in the correct way. They may even repeat their story again and again and provide extra details just to be sure.*

The above information was your guide to telling when someone is lying in person. This is a bit easier than telling that someone is lying from a phone conversation. It can be hard to tell when someone is being deceptive without visual stimuli, but it isn't entirely impossible. Cuts to company budgets have forced some businesses to use the phone for important meetings, instead of meeting in person. Learning and mastering the skill of noticing when someone is lying on the phone is another way to protect yourself from people who will either take advantage or manipulate you for their own selfish gains. This section will cover a few different methods for determining the honesty (or lack thereof) of the person you're speaking with on the phone.

The techniques discussed here will be especially helpful and useful for people who need to give interviews over the phone and select the best candidate for professional reasons. Keep in mind that no psychological method for reading people is right 100 percent of the time, since humans are very complex beings and there are always, without exception, countless factors at play in every human interaction. However, the methods listed here will provide you with somewhere to start, and the ability to detect the probability that someone is being deceptive, not an objective certainty.

- **The Verbal Baseline:** This concept has been discussed in this book a lot, and for good reason; it's highly important when it comes to reading and analyzing people. You can establish a baseline with someone on the phone within a few short minutes. This baseline will consist of paralinguistic and verbal cues from that person. The surest way to establish this is to talk to the person about neutral topics like their name or the weather. You can then notice patterns in the way they speak when they have nothing to hide. After all, why would someone have to lie about the weather?

Later on, as the conversation progresses, you will be able to pay close attention and notice whether or not the person deviates from their normal speech patterns. When someone deviates from their norm, it shows that there is some measure of anxiety present, but there are many different reasons why this could be the case. Deception is only one of those reasons. As mentioned in the previous section about detecting deception, a single deviation doesn't mean that they are lying, and a group of indications is the only way to make an accurate assessment.

- **How long does it Take them to Respond?** People who lie require longer periods of time to answer than people who are truthful and honest. For someone who is truthful, answering a question is a simple process. But liars require extra time for fabricating their answers or trying to make sure they seem honest. The time it takes someone to respond to a "hot" topic question should be compared against the time it took them to respond to neutral, simple questions from the start of the talk. If they take a longer time to answer you, it's possible that they are being deceptive. Honest people might require a *longer period of time to respond if you are asking a thought-provoking question.*

- **The "Well" Trick:** *You can use a technique called the "Well" method for reducing the chance of inaccurately reading someone. When you are asking a person a question that only requires a simple "no" or "yes", and they instead start the sentence with "well," this can be a signal that the person is about to respond with something that they think is unexpected. Keep in mind that this will only work when you are asking someone a simple question that requires a one-worded response.*

- **Using a lot of Filler Words:** *Someone who is lying requires time to come up with answers that they see as believable and acceptable to the person they are attempting to deceive. In order to get some extra time to plan, people who are lying will rely on filler words like "Um," or "uh," before they answer. Another technique that deceptive people will use to get some more time to respond is to either ask for you to repeat what you asked or to respond to your question with their own question. People who are honest will rarely require extra time for answering easy and straightforward questions. And always remember that groups of deceptive signals are always more reliable than just one isolated cue or sign.*

- **Avoidance or Evasive Responses**: People who lie have a hard time giving direct responses, even to questions that are very straightforward. Liars have all sorts of methods and techniques that they will employ to avoid giving direct responses. When you are ever suspecting that someone is lying, simple ask them a question that requires a one-worded answer. If they can't give a response, this heightens the probability that they are lying. If they pause before responded, this is also a slight indication. If they say "Well," first, in addition to the other two cues, this is a highly likely instance that they are lying to you.

Anxiety and Lying

Generally speaking, when someone is being deceptive, they are usually feeling anxious or at least not very comfortable. When you see that someone seems nervous, it's possible that they are lying, but in some cases, it makes more sense that they are simply feeling anxious for some reason. Keep in mind that humans tend to link lying and anxiety together, when this is not always the case. In fact, with people who are very good at lying, they don't feel nervous much of the time. Honest people, on the other hand, might feel very anxious while telling the truth because they are afraid that people might think they are lying.

Conclusion

Thank you again for downloading this book!

I hope this book was able to help you to realize that most of what we say is said outside of speech, and that a person's words are not always a reliable way to interpret how they feel or what they truly think. Once you know how to analyze and read people, you will have a much easier time in all areas of life. Not only will you know what people really think, but you'll be able to communicate what you feel and think in a much clearer way, as well.

The next step is to practice honing these skills until you have perfected them. Start with people who you know quite well and then move onto trying to read people you don't know as well. Finally, if you enjoyed this book, then I'd like to ask you for a favor, would you be kind enough to leave a review for this book on Amazon? It'd be greatly appreciated!

Thank you and good luck!